Text © 2023 by Tracy C. Gold
Illustrations by Nancy Leschnikoff
Cover and internal art and design © 2023 by Sourcebooks

Sourcebooks and the colophon are registered trademarks of Sourcebooks.

The full color art was created using digital mixed media.

Published by Sourcebooks eXplore, an imprint of Sourcebooks Kids
P.O. Box 4410, Naperville, Illinois 60567-4410
(630) 961-3900
sourcebookskids.com

Cataloging-in-Publication Data is on file with the Library of Congress.

Source of Production: Wing King Tong Paper Products Co. Ltd., Shenzhen, Guangdong Province, China
Date of Production: March 2023
Run Number: 5029793

Printed and bound in China.
WKT 10 9 8 7 6 5 4 3 2 1

Hide and Seek, Nuts to Eat

Words by
Tracy C. Gold

Pictures by
Nancy Leschnikoff

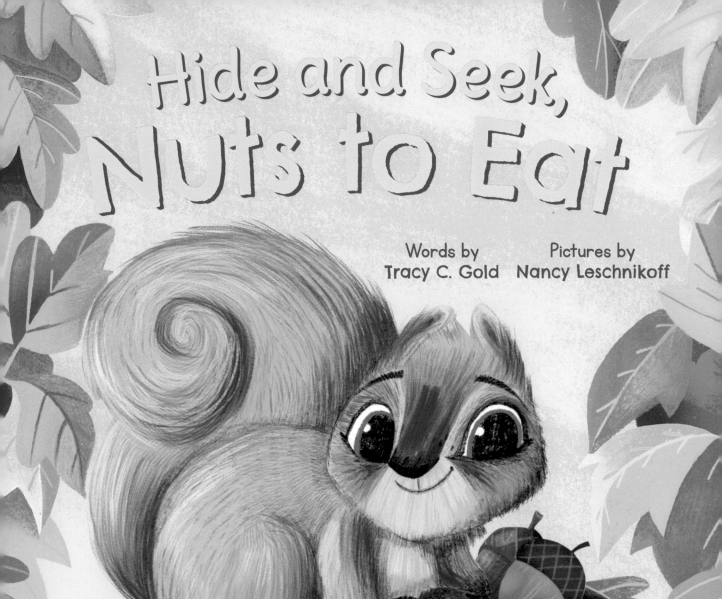

Sourcebooks eXplore

Brrrrr! It's getting colder now.
My coat begins to grow.
Time to start my winter stash
before the freezing snow.

All my friends like stealing food,
which isn't very kind.
I'll be smart and hide a ton
for us to seek and find.

Sniff! I snag some acorns—yum!—
then stash them in the ground.

Next come spinning maple seeds.
I pounce! I leap! I bound!

Whizzing 'round a tall tree trunk,
I'm fast and fab and fleet.
Quick! I grab a hazelnut
while hanging from my feet.

When I'm hungry, I dig up
some tulip bulbs to munch.
Chew 'em, crunch 'em! Hide a bunch
to save for winter lunch.

Eeek! A dog! I dash away.
He barks as up I flee.
"You can't catch me from down there,"
I chirp at him with glee.

Out of reach, a tempting prize—
a juicy berry clump.
I'm a brave and daring squirrel,
so with a squeal, I jump.

Yikes! I fell, but that's okay.
A tumble won't stop me.
Balanced with my bushy tail,
this time I reach the tree!

Bird seeds are my favorite snack.
But then I freeze—a finch!

Birds need food for winter too.
I'll only take a pinch.

Then, one night, a deep snow falls.
The world turns cold and white.

Will we find the treats I hid
to make our dark days bright?

Yes! We seek the food we need
by sniffing all around.
When we smell each little hoard,
we grab it from the ground.

Time to gather in the tree!
We dash in from outside.
Eating berries, nuts, and seeds,
we're cozy warm inside.

What a feast! We eat until
our bellies just might burst.
Then we sip the morning dew
to quench our mighty thirst.

Winter passes... It turns out
from springtime through the fall,
seeds I hid but could not find
start growing big and tall.

Leaves turn brown and pumpkins bulge.
We chomp and chew and squeak!
I made food for everyone
by hiding seeds to seek.

Hiding and Seeking

Tree squirrels survive cold winters by scavenging for food in the fall and saving it for later. Squirrels use their eyes and strong sense of smell to find food like berries, seeds, and nuts. Take a sniff—can you smell any food near you?

Some squirrels, like eastern gray squirrels, dig many holes to hide "caches" of food, which is called "scatter hoarding." Later, these squirrels use their memories and noses to seek their buried food. Scatter hoarding helps protect the food from animals who might take it, like other squirrels, birds, raccoons, deer, opossums, and even bears. Do you have a favorite food that you like to save for later?

Sometimes, squirrels can't find everything they hid, and those seeds buried in the ground turn into new plants. This makes more yummy food for squirrels and also helps keep forests healthy. When seeds are spread out, they compete less for sun and water. Have you seen any surprising plants in your neighborhood? Maybe a squirrel planted them!

If you see a squirrel, don't try to approach it. While a squirrel might forage for food near you, you could scare it if you try to touch it. Enjoy watching squirrels from a comfortable distance.

Sharing (and Stealing!)

Eastern gray squirrels mostly live alone, but they interact with each other a lot. Sometimes they share the same favorite tree or garden to find food—or steal food from each other's caches! Squirrels that are related to each other are more likely to be social. Mother squirrels live with their babies, called kittens, and nurse them. Adult squirrels might groom each other, touch noses, or share nests, called dreys, to stay warm on cold winter nights. What do you like to share with your family and friends?

Squirrels Around the World

There are more than two hundred types of squirrels around the world. Squirrels are rodents, like mice and hamsters. Some squirrel species have always lived in the same place, while other types of squirrels have been introduced to new places by humans. Many types of squirrels look very different from what you might see in a tree near you! What do squirrels look like in your neighborhood?

Eastern Gray Squirrel

Common to North America, these squirrels aren't too picky about what they eat, which means you might see them chowing down on trash. Yuck!

Eurasian Red Squirrel

Tufts of hair make these squirrels' tiny ears look big and pointy. They live in Europe and Asia.

Northern Flying Squirrel

Northern flying squirrels live in forests in North America. They don't flap wings to fly but spread out their loose skin and glide.

Prevost's Squirrel

These squirrels live in Southeast Asia, and one of their favorite foods is coconut.

Sherman's Fox Squirrel

You might see these squirrels in Florida and Georgia. They love to eat pine seeds and use Spanish moss to build their nests.

African Pygmy Squirrel

These tiny squirrels are smaller than a grownup's hand—tail and all. They are found in tropical rain forests in parts of Africa.

Indian Giant Squirrel

Also known as Malabar giant squirrels, these multicolored squirrels are about three feet long if you count their tails. They are commonly found in forests across India.

Barbary Ground Squirrel

Instead of living in the trees, these squirrels dig burrows in the ground in rocky, sandy parts of the Mediterranean and Northern Africa.

Southern Amazon Red Squirrel

Squirrels live in the Amazon rain forest too! These squirrels live mostly on the ground in the undergrowth of South American forests, but they sometimes climb trees.